Jeanine Twigg's

Embroidery Machine ESSENTIALS

Appliqué Adventures

By Mary Mulari

©2006 Mary Mulari

Published by

krause publications

An Imprint of F+W Publications

700 East State Street • Iola, WI 54990-0001
715-445-2214 • 888-457-2873

Our toll-free number to place an order or obtain a free catalog is (800) 258-0929.

Embroidery Design Copyright Information

Library of Congress Catalog Number: 2006929411

ISBN-13: 978-0-89689-405-1

ISBN-10: 0-89689-405-3

Edited by Maria L. Turner and Jeanine Twigg
Designed by Heidi Zastrow and Wendy Wendt

Printed in United States of America

Table of Contents

Foreword

Appliqué is still my favorite embroidery technique, as there are so many creative possibilities. Sure, you can use typical cotton fabrics, but why not do what Mary does? Mary experiments with a variety of other fabrics and fibers and the result is appliqué like no other! She's known for her innovative fabrics and taking appliqué beyond the usual. An appliqué adventure awaits you from the "Appliqué Queen"…my friend, Mary Mulari!

Jeanine

Introduction

Welcome to more appliqué techniques for the embroidery machine. This is my second book in Jeanine Twigg's *Embroidery Machine Essentials* book series and a continuation of ways to enjoy appliqué.

Using a new collection of designs included with this book, you can experiment by combining and altering designs to create appliqués with unique style. We're showing you how to break rules with creative techniques, fibers and textures. There's just no end to the possibilities!

As you page through this book, you'll find a great variety of newfangled ways to embroider appliqués. The CD inside the back cover features 40 embroidery designs to use with your embroidery machine. To experiment with these new embroidery techniques, there are more than a dozen projects with step-by-step instructions. I encourage you to combine the appliqué designs in this book with the designs from my other book in this series, *Embroidery Machine Essentials: Appliqué Techniques*.

It has been a pleasure and an honor to work with Jeanine and contribute to her popular book series. Her creativity, design development and machine expertise have added so much to my own ideas. We are fortunate to have her talents and vision bringing publications and new ideas to sewing and machine embroidery enthusiasts everywhere.

Mary Mulari

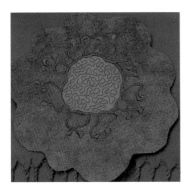

CHAPTER 1

Essentials for Appliqué

Start with the basics and do a little practice-stitching. It won't take long before you've gained the skill and confidence to create appliqués on your embroidery machine. In this chapter, you'll learn about the supplies and techniques to use for successful results. An appliqué adventure begins with a collection of the right supplies and a review of methods that produce professional appliqués, like the large flower decorating this pillow cover.

Why Appliqué?

Appliqué is one of the most popular ways to use an embroidery machine. An appliqué design can stitch faster than solid fill-stitch embroidery designs because fabric covers areas that are usually filled with stitches. It also saves thread for that same reason. This means that instead of replacing thread spools you've emptied, you can spend your thread budget on new colors and types of thread! Mixing embroidery stitches with threads and fabrics of all types increases the design potential and variety.

Designs on the CD

Begin your appliqué adventure by inserting the CD from this book's inside back cover into your computer. When you open the CD, you'll find a folder for each embroidery machine format. Have your machine manual nearby to refer to as you find and copy the appropriate design files to your computer.

Once the designs are on your computer, transfer the designs to your embroidery machine via a jump drive, disk, cable or other media. Most of the designs are for a standard 4" square hoop; however, some of the designs are for a 5" x 7" hoop. For file formats that cannot embroider 5" x 7" designs, the designs will not be shown within the file format on the CD. Should you have any questions about this process, seek help from the sewing machine dealer where you purchased your machine.

Your machine may have a feature that allows you to enlarge or reduce the designs within limitations. Be sure to enlarge designs slightly for using 12-weight embroidery thread. With the aid of embroidery software, you'll be able to combine or edit designs to expand your appliqué adventure.

"Favapron" design on CD.

COPYRIGHT

USING DESIGN SEGMENTS

Ritaswrl   Stitch Count: 1,988   Size: 3.86" x 3.73" (98.0mm x 94.7mm)

   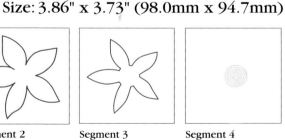 

Segment 1   Segment 2   Segment 3   Segment 4

Each appliqué design is digitized with stitch segments that can be used individually, in sequence to embroider the design completely, or combined with segments of other designs. The Design Details, starting on page 42, shows each appliqué design with the corresponding stitch segments. You will find these reference pages, also printable from the CD, to be of great value as you create your own versions of the designs.

As you embroider each design, the machine will automatically stop between segments. You can change thread colors to begin the next segment, or continue to use the same thread. Preset thread colors shown and listed on the embroidery machine screen may not match your fabric selections, so choose thread colors to match or contrast with your fabrics.

Try combining segments from multiple designs, with a combination of "Dmndcrcl" and "Asterisk" designs on CD.

It's easy to combine segments from more than one design. For example, in the accompanying photo, the "Dmndcrcl" design is combined with segment 9 of the "Asterisk" design placed off-center. The threads chosen for the "Dmndcrcl" segment 4 and 5 are embroidered with variegated 12-weight threads, which provide multiple shades of color throughout the decorative edge stitching.

It's fun to creatively combine designs for appliqué using embroidery software. Use segments from the "Thankyou," "Fllayer" and "Ritastar" designs to experiment with stitch editing, as shown in the accompanying

photo. Rotate the design 90 degrees for the perfect flower and stem design. Use this combined design for one of the many projects introduced in Chapter 4 and detailed on the CD.

Words, a flower and two leaves are combined from three different designs, using the editing options available within your embroidery software, to create the finished look shown.

Supplies You'll Need

As with any project, having basic supplies on hand helps to get embroidering faster. Visit your local sewing machine dealer or find the machine embroidery section of a sewing notions mail-order catalog or Web site to collect not only basic supplies, but also the newest notions and inventions for machine embroidery. Refer to Jeanine Twigg's *Embroidery Machine Essentials* or Nancy Zieman's *Embroidery with Confidence* books for more details and information about supplies you need for embroidery. The following abbreviated list contains the supplies you'll use the most when embroidering appliqué designs.

STABILIZERS

Stabilizers are a necessary part of machine embroidery. They help to support fabrics for embroidery success. After the stitching is complete, tear-away stabilizers can be removed by tearing or cutting around the outside edges of a design, or cut-away stabilizers can be trimmed away and left in place to help to support the embroidery and fabric.

Tear-away stabilizers are used for woven fabrics. Lightweight or medium-weight varieties are usually adequate for appliqué projects. When tearing away the stabilizer after the design is completed, hold your thumb on the stitching lines to support the stitches and carefully tear away from the stitches. Use a curved tip embroidery scissors to catch and lift out the areas of stabilizer from within the design.

Cut-away stabilizers are ideal for knits, fleece and other fabrics that stretch. While the edges of the stabilizer can be cut away, the stabilizer remains to support the stitches and cannot be torn away.

Water-soluble stabilizers are a good choice when you want no signs of stabilizer to remain with the stitching. If a single layer of this stabilizer does not seem adequate, add a second layer.

Another option in this category are adhesive stabilizers with a paper backing. The paper layer is removed to expose the adhesive, which can be adhered to the back of the fabric. After embroidery, the fabric is soaked or laundered to remove all traces of the stabilizer.

Mary recommends: When you need to hold a layer of appliqué fabric to the base fabric, use a temporary spray adhesive to prevent the appliqué fabric from shifting during embroidery. Be sure to spray the appliqué fabric with temporary adhesive in a small box or wastebasket, or over a newspaper away from the embroidery machine and surrounding surfaces.

NEEDLES

A selection of high-quality needles in several sizes will guarantee that you can stitch any embroidery thread with any needle. Standard threads, such as a 40-weight, can be embroidered with a size 11/75 embroidery needle. A size 14/90 embroidery needle is suggested for thicker threads, such as a 30-weight. Use a larger-size topstitching needle, such as a 16/100 or 18/110 for embroidering with 12-weight thread. For metallic threads, use needles specifically designed for use with metallic threads. Titanium embroidery needles are designed for durability and are perfect for use with adhesives because the needle doesn't heat up like standard embroidery needles and therefore won't gum up.

Tip: Change needles frequently when embroidering multiple projects.

"Angel" design on the CD with single-layer dimensional wings.

THREAD

A common choice for typical embroidery is a 40-weight rayon thread. The shine of this thread, particularly in appliqué satin stitches, is elegant and provides a classy edge finish. 30-weight threads are slightly thicker and embroider more prominently.

Consider other types of threads, too. Cotton threads are available in almost every weight imaginable including 12-weight. They provide a matte edge finish and a heavier-weight cotton produces a prominent stitch. Along with solid colors, blended and variegated colors are available, too. When stitching with heavier-weight cotton threads, you may find that enlarging the appliqué design slightly, using a larger size needle and slowing the machine speed will produce successful embroidery results.

Polyester embroidery threads are a good choice for appliqué on items that will be laundered frequently. Metallic threads offer even more shine and glitter than rayon threads. Be sure to use a needle specifically made for use with metallic threads and slow the machine speed during embroidery.

Mary says: To embroider with metallic threads successfully, it can be helpful to use a separate thread-stand away from the machine to allow threads to unwind straight before entering the embroidery machine tension guides. It is also helpful to slow the machine speed during embroidery to allow the needle to penetrate the fabric and form a complete stitch.

SCISSORS

Curved-tip embroidery scissors are the best choice for trimming away fabric inside the embroidery hoop. The tip lifts the appliqué fabric while you are cutting, which prevents cutting the base fabric at the same time. Double-curved scissors, invented just for machine embroidery, allow the curved handle to clear the hoop edge so you can cut more comfortably.

Use a paper scissors to trim and cut stabilizers. Stabilizers will dull the cutting blades of fabric scissors and should not be used for cutting paper-like stabilizers.

Appliqué Guidelines

Appliqué has evolved from hand-guiding sewing machine stitches around fabric shapes to producing the results faster and very professionally on an embroidery machine. The stitches are even and perfectly formed as it embroiders designs with ease.

A few practice sessions will build your confidence and skills in setting up your machine to perform at its best. Experiment with a variety of fabrics, threads and stabilizers. Always use fabrics of good quality and work on base fabrics at least 9" to 12" square. Don't waste your time and thread by working with inexpensive fabric that could never be used to embellish a project.

Also consider fabrics of all colors,

Note how the color of background fabric can change the look of the stitched design, just as it does with "Retrocat" shown here on two different backgrounds.

not just white, for the base fabric for appliqué. Shown in the accompanying photos are the "Retrocat" design stitched on white fabric and again on gold batik fabric. The color of the base fabric and appliqués can enhance a project, depending on your personal preference.

APPLIQUÉ FABRIC CHOICES

While cotton is still a good choice for appliqué, don't be limited to this single category. The samples embroidered for this book include velvet, wool, corduroy, silk, organdy, ribbons, faux suede, flannel, sheers, denim and more. Inspect your fabric collection for unexpected appliqué choices. Just remember that if the item to be appliquéd will be laundered, the appliqué fabric should be washable, too.

Hooping Help

To hoop fabrics and stabilizer, work on a flat surface. Make sure both the fabric and stabilizer are taut and smooth. Hoop and rehoop to get the best and tightest fit, and then tighten the screw on the hoop.

Some fabrics, such as velvet and knits, should not be hooped. Instead, hoop the stabilizer, spray it with temporary spray adhesive and finger-press the fabric to the stabilizer. If additional support is necessary, add pins through the fabric and stabilizer near the edges where embroidery will not stitch. There are alternatives to spray adhesive, such as water-activated or adhesive-back stabilizers. Experiment with a multitude of stabilizers until you are happy with the end results.

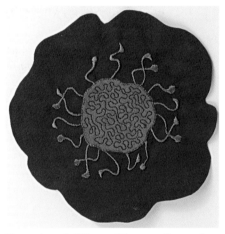

Try stitching the "Flowcntr" design on faux suede for the look shown here. For a creative way to use this sample, check out the Shawl Pillow Cover introduced in Chapter 4 and detailed on the CD.

*Mary says: Do **not** tighten the screw on the hoop after the fabric has been hooped. This will cause puckering around the design. Adjust the hoop screw before the final hooping. Turn the hoop over to make sure the stabilizer is hooped smoothly as well. Ripples in the stabilizer will cause undesirable results.*

APPLIQUÉ EDGE FINISHES

There are several standard raw-edge finishes that you can expect with appliqué designs. Each design-digitizing individual or company produces their appliqués with different steps and raw-edge treatments. Be sure to test-stitch designs or read accompanying literature to determine the steps each digitizer uses for its appliqué designs.

For this book, each step is outlined in the Design Details, starting on page 42. The appliqué is usually one of the first steps, with the edge finish following shortly thereafter. Some appliqués do not have an edge finish and are considered for a raw-edge treatment. Here are some of the typical edge finishes you will find with appliqué techniques.

Satin stitch edge finish shown with additional decorative stitching using the "Moon" design on the CD.

Satin Stitching

With this traditional edge finish, a solid and packed row of threads covers the edges of an appliqué design. Rayon, polyester and metallic threads give a shine to satin-stitched edges; cotton threads have a matte finish. This edge finish is strong and a good choice for covering the edges of easily fraying fabrics.

Raw-Edge Finish

This edge finish does not have extra thread coverage and breaks the rules of traditional appliqué. This choice works well with non-fraying fabrics or fabrics placed on the bias.

For added support to edges that fray, fuse a layer of interfacing to the fabric's wrong side before embroidery. This added support may stop fraying, as well as add body to the fabric weight.

Frayed-Edge Finish

Extra fabric beyond the stitching line is allowed to loosen and fray. To encourage this, use a small brush on the edges and cut off and remove loose threads for a fringed detail on the appliqué.

When using denim for a raw-edge appliqué, allow the laundering process to naturally fray the edges. Cutting the raw edges wider and snipping into the raw edges around the design will help the frayed-edge process.

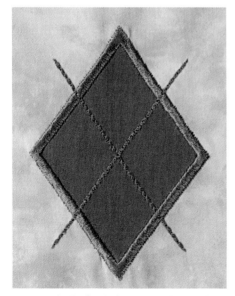

Satin stitch edge finish shown using the "Argyle" design on the CD.

Raw-edge finish shown using segments 1, 2 and 4 of the "Ritaswrl" on the CD.

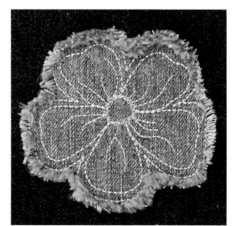

Frayed-edge finish shown using the "Fllayers" design on the CD.

Decorative Stitching

Another nontraditional appliqué choice is creating designs with decorative stitching instead of satin stitches that cover the appliqué. These stitches bring an extra dimension to designs.

Decorative edge finish shown using the "Trees" design on the CD.

Thread Fringe Frames

For a fringy frame around the outer edges of a finished appliqué, like the one around the "Buttrfly" design shown in the accompanying photo, leave extra fabric around the design edge to fray.

Here's how:

1. Hoop the fabric with the stabilizer.

2. Place the hoop on the machine and embroider the design of your choice.

3. Remove the hoop from the machine and remove the stabilizer from the fabric.

4. Trim the fabric edges to within ½", or a length of your choice, around the design.

5. Pull the fabric threads one by one to remove and reveal the fringe. This may take a little time; don't try to pull more than one or two threads at a time. Experiment with heavier fabrics for thicker fringe trim.

Thread fringe frames the "Buttrfly" design, which can be found on the CD.

Cut Fringe Frames

For a cut fringe frame around the outer edge of a finished appliqué, like the one around the "Favapron" design shown in the accompanying photo, snip cuts into the fabric surrounding the design. The trick to this technique is to cut the appliqué fabric on the bias.

Here's how:

1. Hoop the stabilizer and spray it with temporary adhesive.

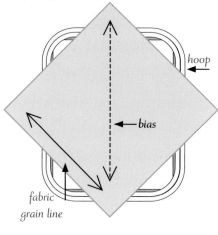

2. Cut an 8" square from fabric and place it "on-point" over the hooped stabilizer, as shown.

3. Place the hoop on the machine and embroider the apron design of your choice.

4. Remove the hoop from the machine and remove the fabric from the hoop.

5. Use a removable marking pen to draw a 4" square centered over the apron design and a 5" square centered over the 4" square.

6. Cut the fabric around the 5" square.

7. Place the square on another piece of fabric or the item you want to decorate.

8. Pin in place and sew the square to the base fabric along the 4" square line.

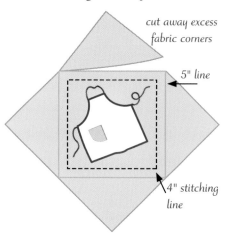

9. Cut the corners from the fabric, on all four sides, leaving approximately ½" framing the design as shown. Then cut fringe down to the stitching line and remove the corner ½" squares as shown in photo. Since the fabric is on the bias, it will not fray.

MARY'S FAVORITE APPLIQUÉ METHODS

I named the appliqué embroidery machine technique "automatic appliqué" because it's easy to achieve the appearance of sewing machine appliqué stitching without all the steps. No more cutting out appliqué shapes, fusing them to the base fabric, determining the perfect appliqué stitch width, and then hand-guiding the sewing machine needle around the appliqué shape. The embroidery machine does most of the work for you!

There are a variety of standard appliqué methods for the embroidery machine—from making templates before embroidering to trimming the appliqué after the outline stitching. Refer to *Embroidery Machine Essentials: Appliqué Techniques* to explore all the appliqué options.

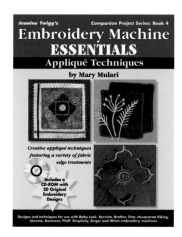

Stitch-and-Trim Appliqué Method

The Stitch-and-Trim Appliqué Method is my favorite for appliqué. It is quick, saves time and there are no templates required.

Here's how (using the standard satin stitch edge finish):

1. Load the "Favapron" design from the CD onto the embroidery machine.

2. Hoop the stabilizer with the fabric.

3. Cut a piece of appliqué fabric large enough to fit inside the hoop.

4. Spray the back of the appliqué fabric with temporary adhesive and place it in the hoop.

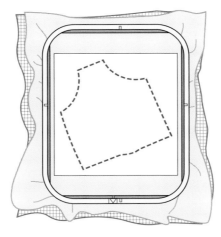

5. Attach the hoop to the machine and embroider segment 1, as shown.

6. Remove the hoop from the machine, but do not remove the fabric from the hoop.

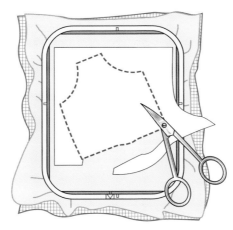

7. Use a curved-tip embroidery scissors to trim away the excess fabric from the outline edges, leaving less than 1/16" of fabric beyond the stitching.

8. Return the hoop to the machine and embroider the remainder of the design. Underlay or zigzag stitches will cover the fabric edges first before satin stitches are embroidered. If the underlay stitches do not completely cover the fabric edges, stop the machine before the satin stitches begin and trim the raw edges again. Be sure to trim close to the underlay stitches. **Note:** Some decorative edge-finishing stitches will not have underlay stitching and may cover the raw edge more efficiently.

9. Remove the hoop from the machine when the appliqué is complete.

10. Remove the fabric and stabilizer from the hoop and remove the stabilizer from the fabric.

11. Press the design on the fabric wrong side using a press cloth and iron.

12. Use the embroidered sample in the Refrigerator Magnet project found in Chapter 4.

Mary says: While trimming fabric, be sure to support the back of the hooped fabric with a flat surface, such as a clipboard or a notebook, to prevent the base fabric from becoming loose in the hoop. It is important to trim very closely so subsequent stitching will cover the entire fabric raw edge. Don't worry if you happen to cut some of the stitches of the outline because the area will be covered by the top stitching. If too much fabric is left beyond the outline stitching, the satin stitches or other topstitching won't cover and threads from the fabric will poke through.

Appliqué in Reverse Method

Instead of placing appliqué fabric on top of the base fabric, this technique places it beneath the base fabric. This technique is a good choice when using delicate appliqué fabrics or fabrics that fray easily.

The two "Heart" designs are shown in the accompanying photos using both techniques. Traditional appliqué is shown on the light green with rust appliqués and reverse appliqué is featured on the rust base fabric with light blue appliqué fabric beneath.

Here's how:

1. Load the "Heart" design from the CD onto the embroidery machine.

"Heart" design created using the Stitch-and-Trim Appliqué Method.

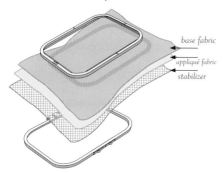

base fabric
appliqué fabric
stabilizer

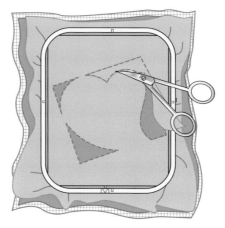

2. Sandwich the appliqué fabric between the stabilizer and the base fabric and hoop all the layers together, as shown.

3. Place the hoop on the machine and embroider segment 1 (appliqué outline).

4. Remove the hoop from the machine, but do not remove the fabric from the hoop.

5. Carefully insert the tip of the curved embroidery scissors into the base fabric only and trim away the base fabric until the appliqué fabric is completely exposed within the outline stitching boundaries.

6. Return the hoop to the machine and embroider the edge-finishing stitches to cover the raw edges and the remainder of the design.

7. Remove the fabric from the hoop and remove the stabilizer.

8. Trim the remainder of the appliqué fabric from the hoop back, close to the edge-finishing stitch.

"Heart" design created using the Reverse Appliqué Method.

MARY'S FAVORITE TIPS

Here are some of my favorite tips that I've found helpful for creating good-looking appliqués. These tips will also save you time and supplies!

Interfacing Appliqués

Many lightweight fabrics need a little extra stability when they're used for appliqué. Fuse a layer of lightweight tricot knit interfacing onto the back of the fabrics before embroidery. The extra stability provides a stronger more even appliqué surface.

Adhesive Stabilizer Economizing

This tip is from Nancy Zieman and her PBS television show "Sewing with Nancy." When using paper-backed adhesive stabilizer for appliqué, the paper can be quite stiff, and it takes some effort to hoop it with the paper side up. This is a way to use smaller pieces of stabilizer while keeping the original stabilizer in the hoop and especially useful for use with larger hoop sizes.

Here's how:

1. Score the paper inside the hoop with a pin and lift off the paper layer to expose the stabilizer.

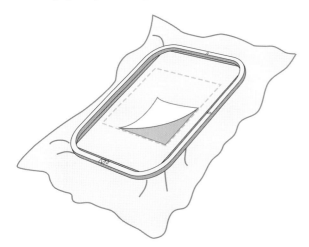

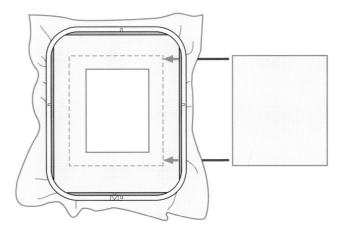

2. Secure the fabric to the adhesive and embroider the design.

3. Use a paper scissors to cut the design carefully from the adhesive layer inside the hoop, leaving the remaining adhesive stabilizer in the hoop.

4. For the next design, cut a piece of the same stabilizer slightly larger than the hole in the stabilizer.

5. Remove the paper backing and adhere the adhesive surface to the bottom of the hoop, over the hole created from the first design.

6. Embroider the next design.

7. Repeat steps 4 through 6 until the original stabilizer does not have enough holding power to keep the base fabric from shifting.

More of Mary's tips are continued on page 16.

Use Pre-wound Bobbins

Pre-filled bobbins are a machine appliqué artist's friend and one of the best timesavers. White and black pre-filled bobbins are readily available, but if you find bobbins in assorted colors, buy them. Be sure to check with your machine dealer to determine if pre-wound bobbin can be used in your machine, and if so, what type. Not all embroidery machines can use pre-wound bobbins, but if they do, you'll love these little timesavers!

Handy Storage

On the table near your embroidery machine, keep a small basket for used thread spools. This prevents the problem of spools falling on the floor or into the wastebasket below. Take the time to secure the loose threads into the spool ends or use a thread wrap to hold the stray thread ends secure.

Snips and Trims

Instead of a wastebasket, use a small paper bag taped to the edge of the sewing table for discarding threads and fabric scraps while embroidering.

Save your adhesive stabilizer excess cuts and hang them from the edge of your sewing table. They're handy for lifting off excess threads and fabric pieces from inside the hoop after trimming away appliqué fabrics. Other products that can be used are pieces of tape, lint remover mitts or a tape-like roller with a handle (a travel size is best for smaller hoops).

Appliqué Trimming Support

For solid support while trimming appliqué fabric in the hoop, use a clipboard. Clamp the base fabric to the board and trim the appliqué fabric away with the hard surface behind the hoop, as shown. This will prevent the scissors from pushing or stretching the hooped fabric, which will then keep the fabric in place and prevent design misalignment during embroidery.

CHAPTER 2

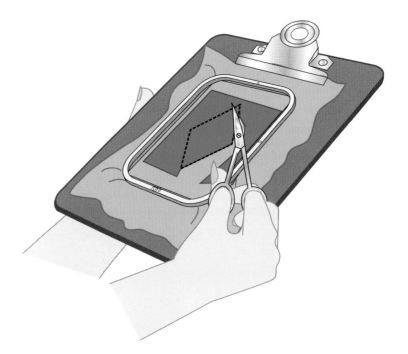

Appliqué Adventures

Appliqué can be much more than a simple, single-layer decoration on a garment. You'll see new possibilities as you page through this chapter. Appliqué appears as closures, pockets, quilt blocks and layered trim. Consider trimming hats, scarves and other accessories with your newfound appliqué creations.

Innovative Techniques

To begin our adventure, let's explore new ways to use appliqué designs — beyond the ordinary. Appliqués can become trims for closures, quilt blocks, pocket trim or can even be fabric-free.

APPLIQUÉS AS POCKETS

Here's a good way to use your appliqué practice pieces as pockets on a tote bag, garments or other accessories. On tote bags, use pockets to conceal a company logo or a stain that won't come out. For the tote bag shown, the "3leafpch" design was used.

Here's how:

1. Plan the appliqué for pocket trim by cutting the base fabric larger and wider than the area to be covered.

2. Embroider the design.

3. Fold back the fabric edges to fit the design into the area on the tote.

4. Cut away excess fabric, leaving 1" for the top pocket hem and ¼" to ½" on the sides and bottom edges to turn under for seam allowances.

5. Add strength to the pocket fabric by fusing lightweight fusible interfacing to the back of the fabric.

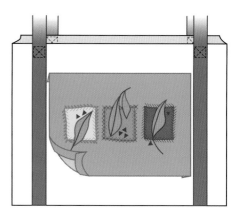

6. Pin the pocket to the tote bag and sew it in place, reinforcing the stitching at the top edges.

STAINED GLASS APPLIQUÉ

"Modleaf" design stitched with black thread to create a stained glass effect.

Achieve the stained glass effect by embroidering using black thread for the "Modleaf" or "Buttrfly" designs on the CD. Embroider the entire design, using hand-dyed watercolor or batik fabrics that have streaks and blotches similar to the appearance of real stained glass as the appliqué. The end result is a stained glass effect.

Maintain a stained glass effect, but get even more creative by using unique fabrics, such as velvet, for the butterfly section of the "Buttrfly" design.

APPLIQUÉS AS CLOSURES

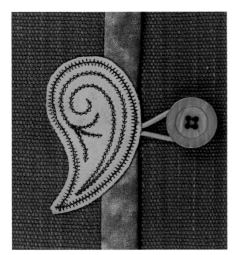

Test the technique of appliqué as a closure using the "Paisleys" design on the CD.

Utilize appliqué designs as a closure trim. You may prefer to reduce the size of the designs to fit within a closure area. Use a ponytail holder as the closure loop surrounding a decorative button.

Here's how:

1. Select firm or non-fraying appliqué fabric. Or, fuse tricot interfacing to the fabric wrong side.

2. Hoop the fabric with water soluble or lightweight tear-away stabilizer.

3. Place the hoop on the machine and embroider the appliqué design.

"Paisleys" design from CD. Segments 1, 2 and 3 were used for this closure techinique.

4. Remove the hoop from the machine and trim the excess fabric away close to the design outermost edges.

5. Decide on the position of the design at the edge of a jacket or other garment.

6. Cut off the metal connector on an elastic ponytail holder before stitching the loop to the garment edge. Sew back and forth to reinforce the stitching over the ponytail holder.

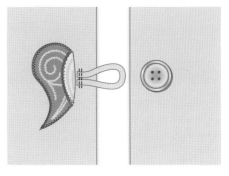

7. Pin and sew the appliqué over the loop ends.

8. Hand-sew a button to the garment's opposite side to make a uniquely trimmed closure.

For another creative appliqué closure idea, see the Button-Up Sweatshirt project introduced in Chapter 4 and detailed on the CD.

QUILTERS' PATCH APPLIQUÉS

Build quilt blocks from appliqué designs, as shown in the accompanying photos. Use leftover project fabrics for the appliqués to color-coordinate with a quilt or wall hanging.

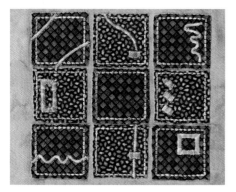

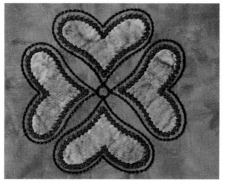

The nine-patch is a traditional quilt pattern. Use the "9patch" design with fabric placed on the bias so cut edges won't ravel. The thread chosen for the project is a 12-weight cotton thread.

The "4hearts" design is reminiscent of a quilt block. This appliqué version is embroidered with 12-weight cotton thread for a prominent edge finish for the shapes.

The "Buttnhls" design (without the buttonholes) makes a traditional pinwheel block. Corduroy fabric placed on the bias adds extra dimension to the half-circle appliqués.

APPLIQUÉS AS EMBROIDERY

The definition of appliqué includes adding one piece of fabric to another. Instead of adding fabric, appliqué designs can be stitched just as embroidery. This is a fast and easy way to use the designs, especially embroidered in all one color.

Appliqués can also be used to quilt layers. Use the outline segments only in any appliqué design for quilting.

"Paisleys" design stitched as an embroidery appliqué.

"Slvrware" design on the CD.

COLORING APPLIQUÉS

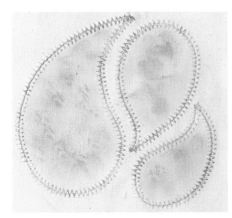

"Paisleys" design shown as a colored appliqué.

"Buttrfly" design colored without dampening the fabric.

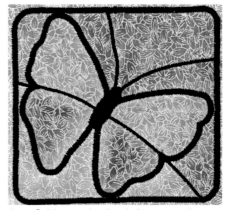

"Buttrfly" design colored with dampening the fabric.

If you enjoy using crayons and coloring books, consider this idea for using appliqué designs to satisfy your love of both embroidery and coloring.

The easiest way to apply color to appliqué designs is to use fabric markers or watercolor paints. Experiment with techniques using test-stitch samples on extra fabric before applying paint to the actual project. When satisfied with the paint colors, iron the design to prevent further bleeding.

Two examples of coloring techniques are shown in the accompanying photos using the "Buttrfly" design. Both samples were embroidered using black thread.

To create a dampened fabric effect, wet the fabric sections between the stitching using a cotton swab. Then, color the areas inside the desired design sections using different-colored fabric markers. The colors will bleed and blend outside each section for a watercolor-effect.

"Modleaf" design was colored one section at a time with different marker colors. Do not paint to the stitch edges of each section. The paint will bleed to cover most of the area within each section. Dampen one section at a time with a wet cotton swab and then color with a fabric marker.

Mary says: Use markers to color plain fabric. Allow the fabric to dry and then use it as appliqué fabric.

Layered Appliqués

We are no longer limited by strict rules for how appliqué should be embroidered, so it's OK to think about lifting the appliqué fabric off the base fabric. There are many different types of dimensional designs. For ease in explaining the varieties, the designs on the CD have been broken into three categories: single, double and triple dimensional layer designs.

SINGLE-LAYER TECHNIQUE

A single-layer dimensional design also can be embroidered with one layer of appliqué fabric <u>off</u> the base fabric and applied to another base fabric with hand or machine-stitches, or by using a button or snap.

Here's how:

1. Load the "4hearts" design onto the embroidery machine.

2. Hoop tear-away stabilizer and spray it with temporary adhesive.

3. Place wool felt centered in the hoop.

4. Place the hoop on the machine and embroider segment 2 (chain stitch heart outlines).

5. Remove the hoop from the machine and remove the fabric from the hoop.

6. Repeat steps 2 through 5 to embroider three more hoopings of hearts using the other colors of wool felt.

7. Tear away the stabilizer after the embroidery is complete. The heart shapes should be soft for use on the knit accessories.

8. Cut the designs from the wool felt. Use a straight scissors or consider pinking shears for a decorative edge.

9. Plan the placement of the hearts on the hat, scarf and gloves. If the knit is very stretchy, designs sewn close together will be spread apart when the accessories are worn.

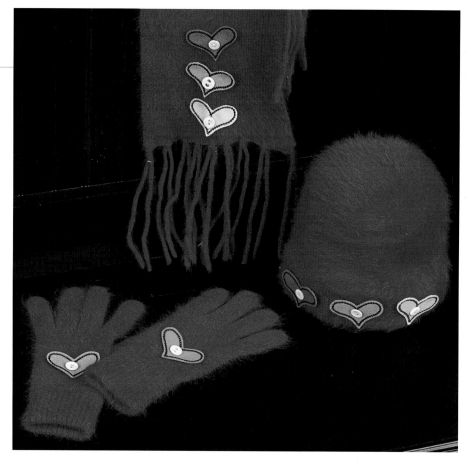

10. Hand-sew small buttons to attach the hearts to the knit accessories.

A single-layer dimensional design can be embroidered with one layer of appliqué fabric <u>on</u> the base fabric.

Here's how:

1. Load the "Coingrid" design onto the embroidery machine.

2. Hoop the base fabric with the stabilizer and embroider segment 1.

3. Cut nine dime-size circles (¾" diameter) using faux suede or another non-fraying fabric.

4. Spray the back of the circles with temporary spray adhesive and position them at the intersections of the stitching lines.

5. Embroider the remainder of the design to secure the circles to the base fabric.

A small button was hand-sewn on to the heart to attach to the knitted accessories.

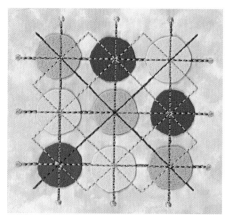

Try the single-layer technique on the base fabric with the "Coingrid" design found on the CD.

DOUBLE-LAYER TECHNIQUE

A double-layer dimensional design can be embroidered with two layers of appliqué fabric <u>on</u> the base fabric, and then embroidered onto the base fabric with other stitches within the design.

Here's how:

1. Load the "Ritastar" design onto the embroidery machine.

2. Hoop water-soluble stabilizer and lightly spray it with temporary adhesive.

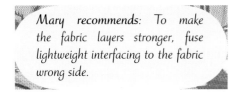

Mary recommends: To make the fabric layers stronger, fuse lightweight interfacing to the fabric wrong side.

3. Secure the fabric to the hooped stabilizer.

4. Place the hoop on the machine and embroider segments 1 and 2 (outline and edge finish).

5. Remove the hoop from the machine and remove the fabric from the hoop.

6. Trim close to the decorative stitching. Remove the stabilizer from the design back.

7. Repeat steps 2 through 6 to embroider segments 4 and 5 (outline and edge finish).

8. To complete the flower, hoop the base fabric with the stabilizer.

9. Embroider segment 1 (outline) using thread to match the base fabric.

10. Place first embroidered flower layer (segments 1 and 2) over the outline.

Mary says: To lift the layer above the base fabric, place a small piece of quilt batting on the base fabric below the center of the flower layer.

11. Embroider segment 4 (outline) using thread to match the appliqué layer.

12. Position the second embroidered flower layer (segments 4 and 5) over the outline.

Mary says: Add a bit of quilt batting beneath the center if you want to lift and separate the layers.

A double-layer dimensional design can be embroidered with two layers of appliqué fabric <u>off</u> the base fabric and applied to another base fabric with hand or machine-stitches, or another layer of appliqué fabric and stitching.

Here's how:

1. Load the "Ritaswrl" design onto the embroidery machine.

2. Hoop medium-weight tear-away stabilizer.

3. Spray the stabilizer with temporary spray adhesive and position felt on the fabric in the hoop.

4. Place the hoop on the machine and embroider the entire design onto wool felt.

5. Remove the hoop from the machine and remove the fabric from the hoop.

6. Repeat steps 2 through 5 to embroider additional flowers. Enlarge or reduce the flower size if desired.

7. Cut around the flower shapes after embroidery, leaving approximately ¼" of fabric beyond the stitching lines.

8. Remove the stabilizer between the cut edge and the stitching, leaving the center of the stabilizer in place. This will help to keep the flowers crisp and firm.

9. Pin the flowers in place on the hat. Hand or machine-sew the flowers to the hat using clear monofilament thread around the edges of the center spiral.

Experiment with this technique using the Guestbook Cover or the Card and Envelope Cover projects introduced in Chapter 4 and detailed on the CD. Two layers of silky fabric backed with fusible interfacing were used to embroider the "Fllayers" flower design on the CD.

TRIPLE-LAYER TECHNIQUE

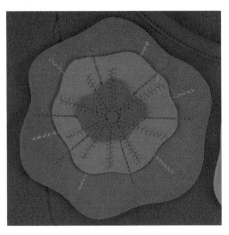

A triple-layer dimensional design can be embroidered with three layers of appliqué fabric off the base fabric and applied to another base fabric with machine-stitches.

Here's how:

1. Load the "Starbrst" design onto the embroidery machine.

2. Print the "Flower" patterns from the CD onto paper. Cut out the patterns and trace the flowers onto the non-fraying fabric. Cut out three layers for each flower.

3. Hoop tear-away stabilizer and spray it with temporary adhesive. Secure the largest flower layer on the stabilizer in the hoop center.

4. Place the hoop on the machine and embroider segment 1.

5. Place the middle flower layer over the largest flower while the hoop is still on the machine and stitch segment 2.

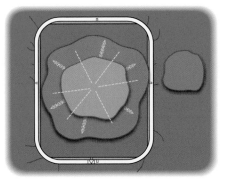

6. Place the smallest flower layer over the middle flower and stitch segment 3.

7. Remove the hoop from the machine and tear away the stabilizer.

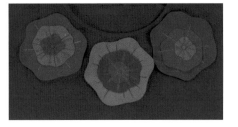

8. Repeat steps 3 through 7 to embroider two more layered flowers.

9. Pin the flowers to the sweatshirt neckline in a pleasing arrangement. Remove the pins before securing the flowers to the sweatshirt.

10. Turn the sweatshirt inside-out and work through the hole in the neck.

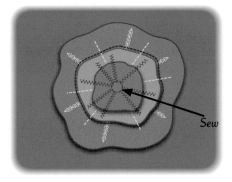

Sew

11. Sew the flower layers to the sweatshirt using the middle flower edge as a guide. Only sew through the largest flower layer.

Overlays and Backgrounds

Adding embroidery or fabrics over or under appliqué is a unique way to add texture to embroidery. Whether the overlay is fabric or stitches, experiment with layering techniques that do not follow traditional appliqué guidelines.

SHEER FABRIC OVERLAYS

Choose bright-colored fabrics for the appliqués and add a top layer of sheer fabric or tulle to soften the colors. You can see the change to the appliqué fabrics when the sheer fabric is placed over the design.

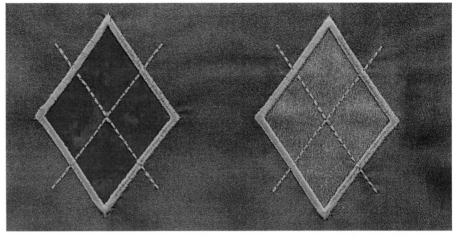

"Argyle" design shown stitched with bright red fabric (left) and then with a sheer fabric over the bright red (right). Notice what a different look is created by placing a sheer fabric overlay on the original design.

EMBROIDERY OVERLAYS

Traditional appliqués require edge finishes. Try a unique technique of stitches that overlays the appliqué area where fabric is placed. Scatter embroidery stitches, crystals, beads or other ornamental accents on the fabric for additional flair.

Here's how:

1. Hoop the stabilizer with the base fabric.

2. Cut a design shape or position random scraps of fabric within the design area.

> *Mary says: Use shapes cut on the bias, as they will not ravel.*

3. Spray the back of the appliqué pieces with temporary spray adhesive and position them inside the hoop.

4. Select a background or stitch pattern to embroider over the appliqué pieces.

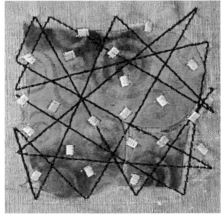

The "Scrubdot" design shown stitched using the technique of stitching over the appliqué area where fabric is placed.

The "Twigssm" design was embroidered over an assortment of cut wool triangles scattered on the base fabric. Spray the back side of the triangle with temporary adhesive to hold them in place during embroidery. Use a lightweight, tear-away water-soluble stabilizer over the cut pieces if the pieces get caught in the stitching. Tear away the stabilizer after embroidery.

USING BACKGROUNDS

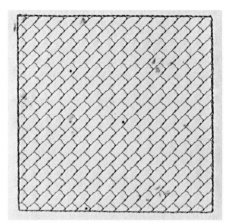

One of several background embroidery designs found on the CD that can be used specifically for backgrounds or as embroidery designs on their own.

There are five background designs on the CD and two satin stitch frame designs. These seven files are created to work together. Embroider the background designs and use them as a background behind an appliqué design, use them as an appliqué design on their own or use them with the satin stitch frames as a pocket shown in the Pursonalities project introduced in Chapter 4 and detailed on the CD.

Background design used with the satin stitch frame for the pocket on the Pursonalities project.

For a pronounced appearance to the stitching, use a heavier-weight cotton 30- or 12-weight embroidery thread and a larger needle. Slow the machine speed to allow the stitches to form on the fabric.

The accompanying satin stitch frames are available to finish the edges of the backgrounds. Embroider the backgrounds on separate fabric and use the satin stitch frames as appliqué.

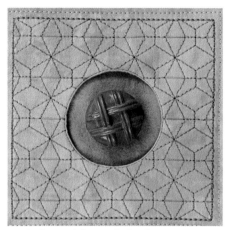

Use background designs for faced openings featured on page 30.

CHAPTER 3

More Appliqué Adventures

In case you thought that cotton fabric was the only choice for appliqué, study this chapter to widen your stitching horizons. You'll find ways to alter fabric surfaces with gathers, pleats and weaving. Just as the title of this book promises, this is an appliqué adventure!

To continue your adventure with appliqué, let's move away from the traditional flat fabric and add in some texture to your designs. This chapter shows ways to use innovation for more interesting appliqué accents.

Altered Fabric Appliqués

What else can we do to appliqué fabrics that will add even more interest to embroidery? Let's keep the adventure going!

GATHERS

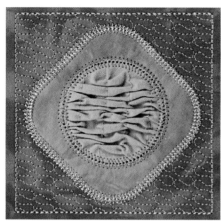

Texturize appliqué fabric by adding gathers before embroidery using the "Dmndcrcl" design found on the CD.

Here's how:

1. Cut a 5" square of fabric for the appliqué.

2. Set the sewing machine stitch length to basting.

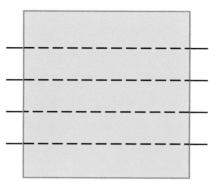

3. Sew lines of basting stitches about ½" apart, or set the spacing to your preference.

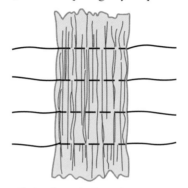

4. Pull the threads from both fabric edges after the lines are sewn to form the gathers.

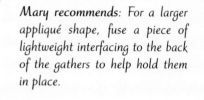

Mary recommends: For a larger appliqué shape, fuse a piece of lightweight interfacing to the back of the gathers to help hold them in place.

5. Use the gathered fabric as an appliqué when stitching segment 4 of the "Dmndcrcl" design or in the reverse appliqué technique on page 14 to cover the raw edges completly. For best results, embroider the outline around the appliqué twice to secure it to the base fabric, as it will be bulky due to the gathers.

Mary says: These Altered Fabric techniques affirm the belief that you need to have at least two machines: one to sew and one to embroider!

PLEATS

Fold and press narrow pleats into fabric and incorporate the altered fabric into an appliqué design. Soft, light fabric is best to avoid bulk when embroidering the appliqué. Once you've mastered the basic technique below, continue with the pleat adventure by folding irregular pleats or stitching an embroidery design on the pleats themselves for more interest.

Here's how:

1. Place the wrong side of a 4" x 8" piece of fabric facing up. Fold and press narrow pleats into the fabric to cover the appliqué area. Use a pleater board if desired.

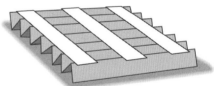

2. Press the pleats gently and fuse strips or a solid piece of lightweight fusible interfacing over the pleat wrong side, as shown. Or, sew across the pleat edges to hold them in place.

3. Use the pleated fabric as an appliqué when embroidering segments 1 through 4 of the "Asterisk" design. For best results, embroider the outline around each appliqué twice to secure it to the base fabric, as it will be bulky due to the pleats.

WEAVING

Cut bias strips of fabric and weave them with bias tape, ribbon, twill tape, or trim. You'll be creating an unusual fabric for an appliqué.

Here's how:

1. Place fabric strips right sides down, pinning them to a padded surface, such as an ironing board.

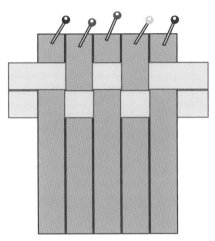

2. Weave additional strips horizontally through the vertical strips, as shown, using enough strips to create a woven piece large enough for the appliqué.

3. Fuse a piece of lightweight fusible interfacing to the wrong side of the woven appliqué to secure the strips in place.

4. Use the woven fabric as an appliqué when embroidering segment 1 of the "Modleaf" design. For best results, embroider the outline around each appliqué twice to secure it to the base fabric, as it will be bulky due to the weaving layers.

NEEDLE FELTING

Choose a felt, wool or a knit for the base fabric and add felt or wool shapes for the appliqués. The barbed needles of the hand tool or the Embellisher machine from Baby Lock push the top fabric into the bottom fabric to create patterns and unique textures. Stitches added to the top of the felted fabrics secure the top pieces and add an extra touch of embellishment

Here's how:

Push the fibers of appliqué fabric into the base fabric with a needle felting tool or by using the Embellisher machine. The large flower was created from layers of felt and yarn trim. The stitching detail was added to the design after it was felted. To best stitch through areas of heavily felted layers, use a 110 size topstitching or jeans needle to pierce the fabrics.

FACED OPENINGS

Use of the background designs on the CD to embellish a piece of fabric, and then create a faced frame for another embroidery design or a decorative button. There is a lot of dimension and interest in these frames.

Here's how:

1. Hoop stabilizer with base fabric

2. Place the hoop on the machine and embroider one of the background designs.

3. Remove the hoop from the machine and remove the fabric from the hoop.

4. Remove the stabilizer from the fabric that is extending beyond the outer edges of embroidery design.

5. Embroider a small appliqué design, such as the "Gingko" leaf on another piece of fabric. Reduce the design size 20 percent, if necessary.

6. Trace a circle or another shape on the wrong side of the background design larger than the embroidered small design or item you wish to frame. It can be in the center of the design area or off-center.

7. Cut a 5" square fabric piece for the frame lining.

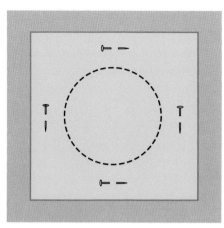

8. Place both fabrics right sides together and sew around the circle or shape.

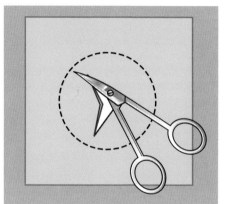

9. Cut the shape out of both layers of fabric, as shown, leaving a ¼" seam allowance. Clip seams, if necessary.

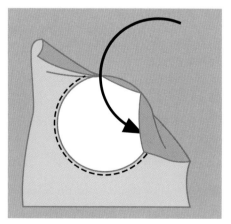

10. Bring the lining fabric to the wrong side of the background design and press the opening and lining fabric flat.

11. Position the small appliqué design centered in the opening, as shown.

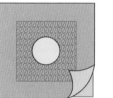

12. Pin the layers together and sew around the outside of the embroidery design with the same thread used for embroidery. Use a straight stitch or a decorative sewing machine stitch.

13. Optional: For a faced button frame, cut a 5" piece of fabric for the opening and follow step 12 above. Hand-sew a button in the opening.

Another example using a faced opening with a button on the "Bckgrnd5" design found on the CD.

Innovative Fibers

Look beyond your fabrics for appliqué possibilities. Experiment with new fibers, such as paper, petals and yarn.

PAPER

Embroidered appliqué on paper is featured on the Thank You Card project introduced in Chapter 4 and detailed on the CD.

Experimenting with paper instead of fabric for appliqués is a fun change from the ordinary. The nice thing about paper is that it doesn't ravel, yet it can be very fragile. So, test-stitching is a must for embroidering on paper. Consider purchasing an abundant supply of each paper type (bulk packaging is great), or purchase at least three of each paper sheet for testing and the real project.

Outline, quilting and appliqué designs make for great paper creations. Depending on the digitizing company, it may be necessary to enlarge designs without stitch count changes to ensure there is enough space between stitches to prevent perforating the paper. Satin stitches may not hold up well to embroidery on paper and may perforate the paper if not stabilized well. For best results, use an open design without a lot of stitches.

Depending on the paper, use an appropriate needle to work with the embroidery thread chosen. For example, if a heavyweight paper and 12-weight thread is chosen, use a 16/100 or 18/110 needle for embroidery. Be sure to slow the machine speed as you would for fabric. Slowing the machine speed will enable the needle to penetrate the paper and allow the thread to form complete stitches.

For more information and project ideas for embroidering on paper, check out Annette Gentry Bailey's book *Machine Embroidery on Paper* published by Krause Publications.

Mulberry Paper

"Heart" design stitched on Mulberry paper background.

This lovely paper has streaks of fibers running through it, making it easy to embroider outline designs without a stabilizer.

Here's how:

1. Fold an 8½" x 11" sheet in half to make a 5½" x 11" sheet.

2. Hoop the paper so the left and right sides of the inner and outer hoop hold the paper in place during embroidery.

3. Slow the machine speed for best results and stitch the design.

Another option is to hoop a piece of lightweight tear-away stabilizer, spray it with adhesive and embroider an appliqué design with a single layer of cotton fabric as shown. The additional fabric fibers in this paper aids in successful embroidery.

Cardstock

"Coingrid" design on the CD.

A heavier-weight paper is perfect for embroidery, as it holds the stitches with ease.

Here's how:

1. Hoop a sheet of lightweight tear-away stabilizer, spray it with temporary adhesive and secure the cardstock to the stabilizer.

2. Embroider an outline design with another piece of paper as the appliqué.

3. Tear away the stabilizer after embroidery.

4. Depending on the design, the paper appliqué can be torn away from the outline stitching, as long as another series of stitches embroider over the appliqué to hold it in place.

For a more secure application, use an adhesive tear-away stabilizer to hold the paper firmly secure. Do not attempt to tear away the stabilizer after embroidery; keep the stabilizer adhered to the paper for added support by cutting it to fit the size of the paper.

ANGELINA FIBERS

"Ritastar" design on the CD.

These innovative sparkly fibers make great appliqué fabric. The fibers are available mixed with a bonding agent that, when ironed, turn into an iridescent material perfect for appliqué.

Here's how:

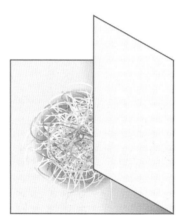

1. Place the fibers between two layers of a nonstick appliqué pressing sheet, as shown.

2. Use a dry iron to heat the fibers. The fibers will bond together to form a thin sheet of material perfect for appliqué. For best results, follow the manufacturer's instructions that accompany the fibers.

3. Use the bonded Angelina Fibers as you would any fabric for an appliqué. (The two layers of the "Ritastar" appliqué shown in the accompanying photo have been created using Angelina Fibers. The appliqués from the fibers were easy to sew and cut.)

FLOWER PETALS

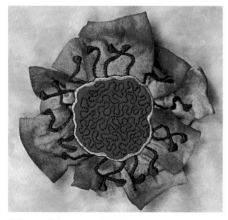

"Flowcntr" design on the CD.

Use petals from silk flowers or use Bella Nonna silk petals to create an appliqué flower, or to trim the edges of a design.

Here's how:

1. Hoop the base fabric with the stabilizer.

2. Stitch the appliqué outline.

3. Arrange the petals over the edge of the outline.

4. Embroider the appliqué outline again so it will secure the petals to the base fabric. Be sure to slow the machine speed during this step. Because the petals do not easily lie flat, you may find that taping the outer edge to the base fabric will help to keep them in position during step 4 embroidery.

5. Place the appliqué fabric over the design area and stitch the outline stitch one more time (this will be the third time).

6. Take time to carefully trim away the excess fabric around the appliqué. Watch out for the petals underneath to avoid cutting them.

7. Finish embroidering the design segments desired.

"Heart" design on the CD.

YARN

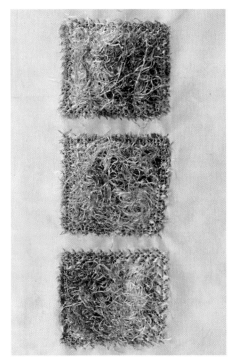

"3leafpch" design stitched on knitted yarn blocks.

Knitting and crocheting will never go out of style. The luscious yarns and cozy feel are perfect for your appliqué adventure. For every knitting or crochet project, a sample is made to obtain the gauge. Why not use those leftover gauge samples for appliqué designs? Or, if you don't knit or crochet and have a friend who does, ask to use her gauge samples when she is finished with a project.

Knit and purl sides of knitting.

There are two sides of a knitted sample—the knit side and the purl side. Depending on the yarn, perhaps the knit side is more usable as an appliqué than the purl side of the sample. It doesn't matter which side is used. Look at each side to determine which you prefer for the appliqué.

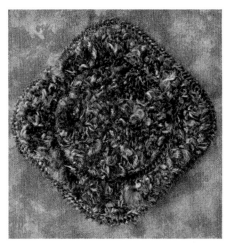

Segment 2 and 4 of "Dmndcrcl" on the CD.

Experiment with a variety of knit or crochet yarns. Some yarns are bulky, which means they have a loft when knitted or crocheted. These samples may require the use of a water-soluble stabilizer topper to temporarily hold lofty fibers in place during embroidery. Each yarn will produce appliqués differently. Experiment by stitching a variety of samples to obtain a general idea of how yarns will look for appliqué.

Use the knit or crochet sample in an appliqué design as you would for fleece or another lofty fabric. For best results, stitch the appliqué outline twice before embroidering the edge-finishing stitches.

LOOSE THREADS

"Buttrfly" design on the CD.

Why not use your leftover snips of threads, yarns and fibers for appliqué? Sandwich the fibers between two layers of water-soluble stabilizer and embroider one of the background designs on the CD. Be sure all the fibers used in the appliqué sandwich are washable. Rinse the stabilizer from the fibers and use the fibers in an appliqué.

Here's how:

1. Sandwich snips of thread, fabric or other fibers between two layers of cut-away, water-soluble stabilizer. Keep the fibers confined to ½" larger than the appliqué design area.

2. Or, hoop a layer of cut-away, water-soluble stabilizer and place the snippets of fibers into the hoop area. Place the other layer of cut-away, water-soluble stabilizer on top of the fibers. Use hand- or machine-basting stitches to hold the layers together.

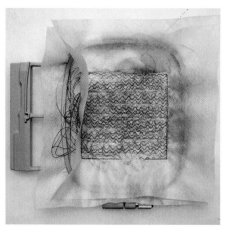

3. Place the hoop on the machine and embroider the background design of your choice with variegated polyester embroidery thread.

4. Remove the hoop from the machine and remove the fabric from the hoop.

5. Rinse the embroidered threads in tepid water until the water-soluble stabilizer is completely removed from the fibers.

6. Use the embroidered threads in an appliqué as you would any other fabric.

CHAPTER 4

Inspirational Project Ideas

To help you experiment with the techniques featured in this book, here are 12 creative ways to use appliqué designs. Try a new project each month for a year's worth of appliqué adventures. Learn how to combine designs, trim a place mat with appliqués and turn it into a purse, start a new holiday tradition with Christmas mittens, and lots more. Start by turning a sweatshirt into a cardigan and adding buttonhole closures using the "Buttnhls" appliqué designs found on the CD. There is truly no end to the possibilities for appliqué, so let these projects inspire your creative spirit.

Detailed step-by-step instructions for completing all of the projects are located on the CD.

Christmas Mittens

Initiate a new tradition with mittens instead of stockings hanging from the fireplace mantel at Christmas. These generously sized mittens will hold plenty of gifts including CDs and other larger-sized packages. The mittens are made from heavyweight wool and decorative trim encircles the cuffs. Embroider the "Snowflke" design found on the CD at the tips of each mitten. You'll find the mittens are easy to embellish and sew for the perfect holiday decoration.

It's a Wrap!

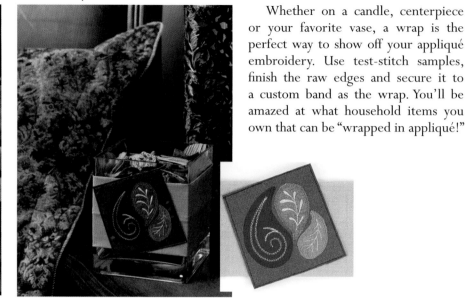

Whether on a candle, centerpiece or your favorite vase, a wrap is the perfect way to show off your appliqué embroidery. Use test-stitch samples, finish the raw edges and secure it to a custom band as the wrap. You'll be amazed at what household items you own that can be "wrapped in appliqué!"

Reversible Apron

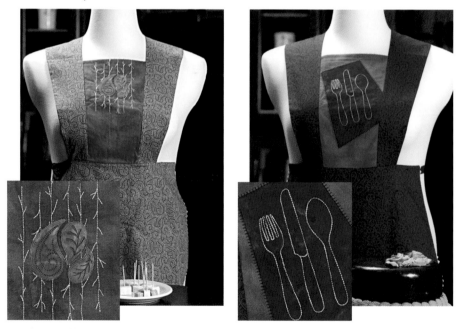

Show off two appliqué techniques by trimming both bib sections of this reversible apron, which is the Blue Ribbon Apron from my pattern, "Newfangled Reversible Aprons." Two designs are combined on the bib shown: the large twigs and the paisley designs. Stitching the designs on a piece of fabric larger than the bib pattern allows placement decisions to be made after the stitching is complete; cutting the bib pattern from see-through material such as quilting template plastic makes it easy to place the embroideries exactly where you want them. Side 2 of the bib features the 5" x 7" silverware design stitched on a large piece of fabric that is then placed off-center on the bib fabric. The fabric piece could also be sewn to the bib as a pocket to hold a recipe card, reading glasses or a portable digital music player.

Guardian Angel Pillowcase

Buy or sew a pillowcase and make it special with the addition of an appliquéd pocket. The "Angel" design found on the CD is an appropriate choice for someone staying in the hospital or experiencing health problems. After embroidering the design, select two coordinating fabrics to sew to the pillowcase as patches or frames for the pocket. Before you present the decorated pillowcase as a gift, add a note of good wishes inside the pocket.

Kitchen Wall Hanging

Apron appliqués are perfect trim for a kitchen wall hanging. Coordinate the fabric colors with your kitchen decor. The appliquéd squares are sewn to the background fabric as patches. The vinyl pocket in the center holds a recipe for the day's meal or one of special meaning. The recipe card in the pocket shown features one of my mother's favorite recipes in her own handwriting. You'll find this project quick and easy to complete plus a terrific gift idea.

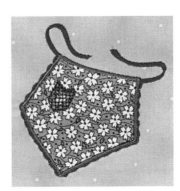

Shawl Pillow Cover

Appliqué is a perfect accent for decorations in the home. A fabric shawl with an interesting fringe trim can be turned into an envelope-style pillow cover for a 16" pillow form. The large floral faux suede appliqué adds extra interest to the fringed edge.

Postcard Greetings

Sending a custom-made postcard through the mail is a great way to show someone you care. Embellish fabric with an appliqué or use a test-stitch sample, adhere the fabric to cardstock with permanent spray adhesive and send the postcard in the mail. Don't forget the postage! A 4" x 6" standard-size postcard—no matter how fancy—can be mailed at the standard postcard rate. Be sure to have your local postmaster "hand-cancel" the postcard to prevent it from going through automatic equipment. If you want to protect the decorative surface from postal wear and tear, insert the postcard into a closely sized close-top bag and take it to the post office to mail. The postmaster will secure the postage to the outside of the bag and hand-cancel it for smooth sailing.

Thank You Card

Embroidery and appliqué with paper is a fun alternative to fabric. The outline shapes built into appliqué designs are perfect for embroidering onto paper. From mulberry to cardstock, use a lot of the same techniques as you would for fabric, instead just use paper. The difference is that paper can be fragile. Therefore, slow the machine speed and take care in using the appropriate stabilizers. In most cases, a tear-away stabilizer and temporary spray adhesive is all you need for successful embroidery on paper. Experiment with paper appliqué with this project.

Creative Covers

Covering a scrapbook, guest book or a journal is simple especially when it is embroidered with the perfect appliqué designs. Embroider a guest book and place it on an entry way table for guests to sign as they come and go throughout the years. This is the perfect gift-giving idea for someone with a new home or cottage. As the years pass by, it is a wonderful reminder of those who have come to visit. Show off your embroidery creativity by making stationery covers from faux suede to give to guests for a reminder of their visit with you. It is in our nature to give, so why not give with an expression of your creativity?

Pursonalities

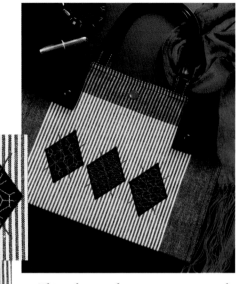

This classy, clever purse is made from a reversible fabric place mat. Table linens are getting fancier and so is the construction! No longer are place mats just for the kitchen or dining room; they are a blank slate for appliqué embroidery! The shape of a place mat when folded is perfect for a handbag. The added "stiff" interfacing will help reinforce the fabric for the contents you'll be carrying. Add inside pockets before assembly using monofilament sewing thread in the needle and bobbin. And make a pocket on the outside to hold a cell-phone, using the embroidery designs on the CD.

Refrigerator Magnet

The refrigerator is the hub of any busy family and this handy pouch is perfect for a pad of note paper and pen. No more searching for the supplies to write a quick note. Whether the notes are for groceries or to alert family members of your whereabouts, they'll love the magnetic pouch you made with love.

Button-Up Cardigan

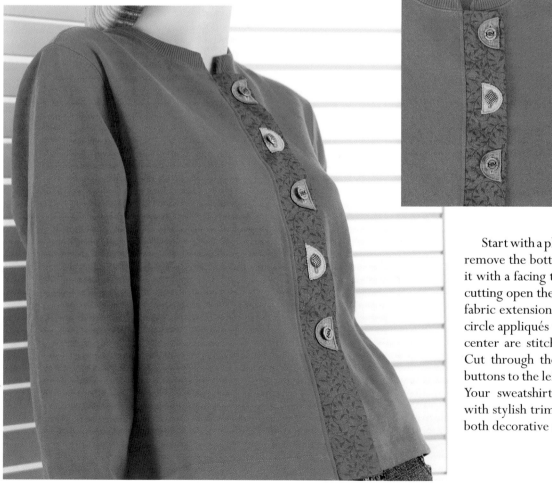

Start with a plain pullover sweatshirt, remove the bottom ribbing and replace it with a facing to finish the edge. After cutting open the sweatshirt front, add a fabric extension to the right side. Half-circle appliqués with buttonholes in the center are stitched to the fabric strip. Cut through the buttonholes and add buttons to the left side of the sweatshirt. Your sweatshirt has become a jacket with stylish trim and appliqués that are both decorative and functional.

Resources

Look for these and other embroidery products at a local retailer where embroidery machines, software, and designs are sold. To find a dealer near you, contact these companies of interest.

SUPPLIES

Bella Nonna Design Studio (silk flower petals)

509-374-4369
www.bellanonnaquilt.com

Mary's Productions (Mary Mulari)

218-229-2804
www.marymulari.com

Nancy's Notions

800-833-0690
www.nancysnotions.com

PUBLICATIONS

Creative Machine Embroidery

800-677-5212
www.cmemag.com

Designs in Machine Embroidery

888-SEW-0555
www.dzgns.com

Embroidery Journal

480-419-0167
www.embroideryjournal.com

Sew News

800-289-6397
www.sewnews.com

EMBROIDERY MACHINE COMPANIES

Baby Lock

800-422-2952
www.babylock.com

Bernina

800-405-2739
www.berninausa.com

Brother

800-422-7684
www.brothersews.com

Elna

800-848-3562
www.elnausa.com

Husqvarna-Viking Sewing Machines

800-358-0001
www.husqvarnaviking.com

Janome

800-631-0183
www.janome.com

Kenmore

888-809-7158
www.sears.com

Pfaff

800-997-3233
www.pfaffusa.com

Simplicity

800-553-5332
www.simplicitysewing.com

Singer

800-474-6437
www.singershop.com

White

800-311-3164
www.whitesewing.com

Design Details

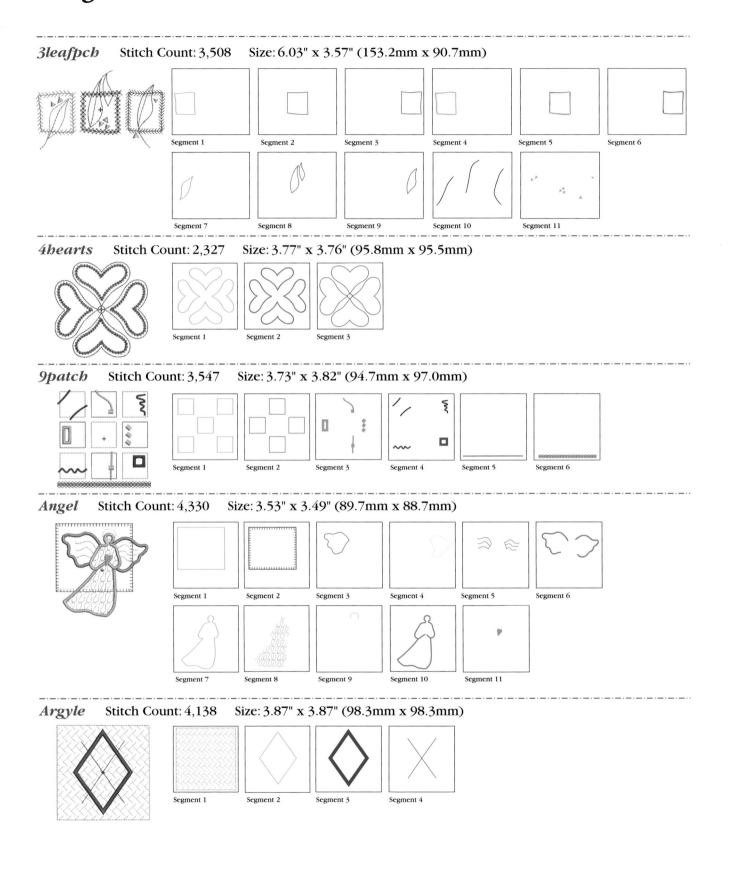

3leafpch Stitch Count: 3,508 Size: 6.03" x 3.57" (153.2mm x 90.7mm)

Segment 1 Segment 2 Segment 3 Segment 4 Segment 5 Segment 6

Segment 7 Segment 8 Segment 9 Segment 10 Segment 11

4hearts Stitch Count: 2,327 Size: 3.77" x 3.76" (95.8mm x 95.5mm)

Segment 1 Segment 2 Segment 3

9patch Stitch Count: 3,547 Size: 3.73" x 3.82" (94.7mm x 97.0mm)

Segment 1 Segment 2 Segment 3 Segment 4 Segment 5 Segment 6

Angel Stitch Count: 4,330 Size: 3.53" x 3.49" (89.7mm x 88.7mm)

Segment 1 Segment 2 Segment 3 Segment 4 Segment 5 Segment 6

Segment 7 Segment 8 Segment 9 Segment 10 Segment 11

Argyle Stitch Count: 4,138 Size: 3.87" x 3.87" (98.3mm x 98.3mm)

Segment 1 Segment 2 Segment 3 Segment 4

Asterisk   Stitch Count: 4,271   Size: 3.70" x 3.70" (94.0mm x 94.0mm)

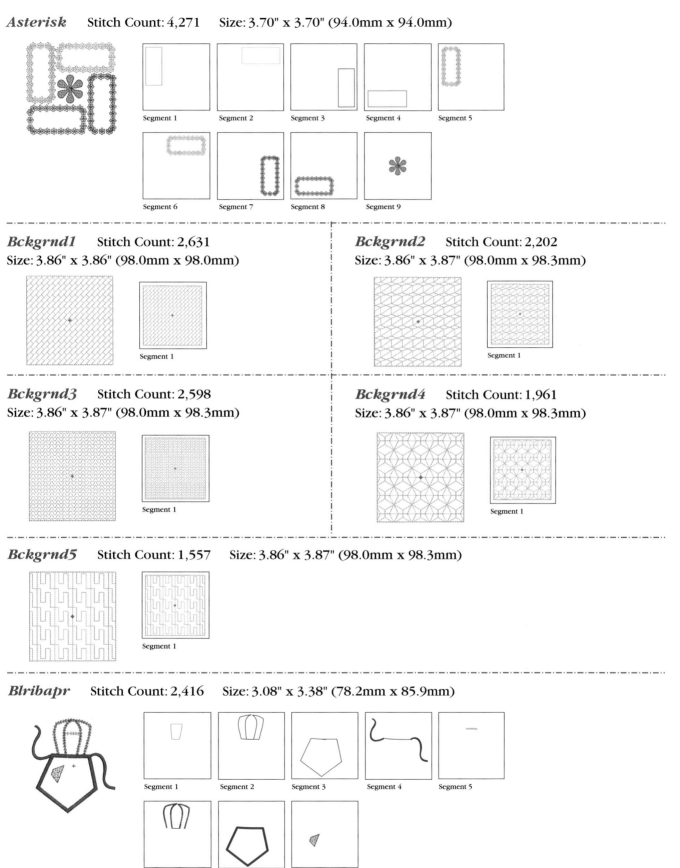

Segment 1   Segment 2   Segment 3   Segment 4   Segment 5

Segment 6   Segment 7   Segment 8   Segment 9

Bckgrnd1   Stitch Count: 2,631
Size: 3.86" x 3.86" (98.0mm x 98.0mm)

Segment 1

Bckgrnd2   Stitch Count: 2,202
Size: 3.86" x 3.87" (98.0mm x 98.3mm)

Segment 1

Bckgrnd3   Stitch Count: 2,598
Size: 3.86" x 3.87" (98.0mm x 98.3mm)

Segment 1

Bckgrnd4   Stitch Count: 1,961
Size: 3.86" x 3.87" (98.0mm x 98.3mm)

Segment 1

Bckgrnd5   Stitch Count: 1,557   Size: 3.86" x 3.87" (98.0mm x 98.3mm)

Segment 1

Blribapr   Stitch Count: 2,416   Size: 3.08" x 3.38" (78.2mm x 85.9mm)

Segment 1   Segment 2   Segment 3   Segment 4   Segment 5

Segment 6   Segment 7   Segment 8

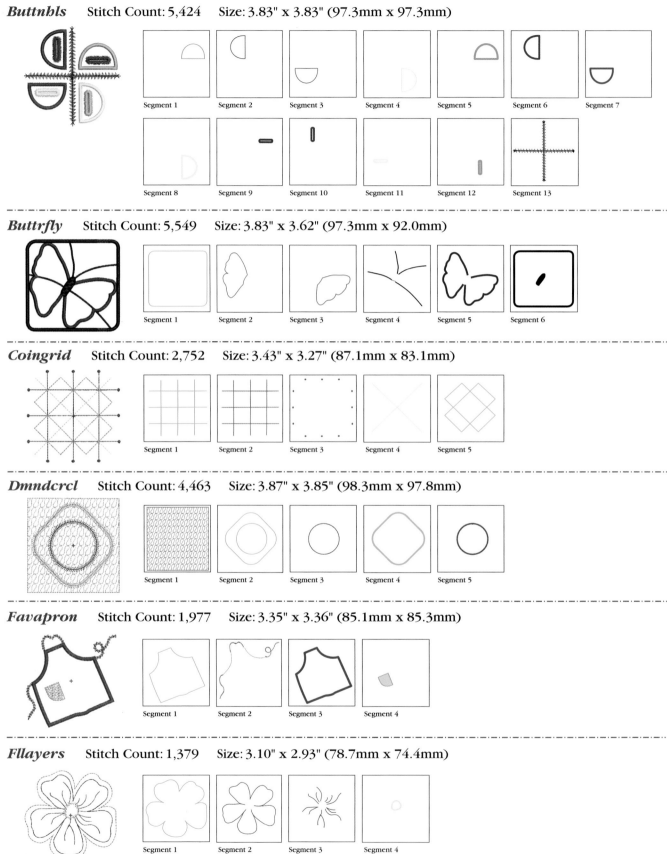

Buttnhls   Stitch Count: 5,424   Size: 3.83" x 3.83" (97.3mm x 97.3mm)

Segment 1   Segment 2   Segment 3   Segment 4   Segment 5   Segment 6   Segment 7

Segment 8   Segment 9   Segment 10   Segment 11   Segment 12   Segment 13

Buttrfly   Stitch Count: 5,549   Size: 3.83" x 3.62" (97.3mm x 92.0mm)

Segment 1   Segment 2   Segment 3   Segment 4   Segment 5   Segment 6

Coingrid   Stitch Count: 2,752   Size: 3.43" x 3.27" (87.1mm x 83.1mm)

Segment 1   Segment 2   Segment 3   Segment 4   Segment 5

Dmndcrcl   Stitch Count: 4,463   Size: 3.87" x 3.85" (98.3mm x 97.8mm)

Segment 1   Segment 2   Segment 3   Segment 4   Segment 5

Favapron   Stitch Count: 1,977   Size: 3.35" x 3.36" (85.1mm x 85.3mm)

Segment 1   Segment 2   Segment 3   Segment 4

Fllayers   Stitch Count: 1,379   Size: 3.10" x 2.93" (78.7mm x 74.4mm)

Segment 1   Segment 2   Segment 3   Segment 4

Flleaves   Stitch Count: 1,717   Size: 6.20" x 4.06" (157.5mm x 103.1mm)

Segment 1

Flowcntr   Stitch Count: 7,040   Size: 3.59" x 3.48" (91.2mm x 88.4mm)

Gingko   Stitch Count: 4,960   Size: 3.53" x 3.51" (89.7mm x 89.2mm)

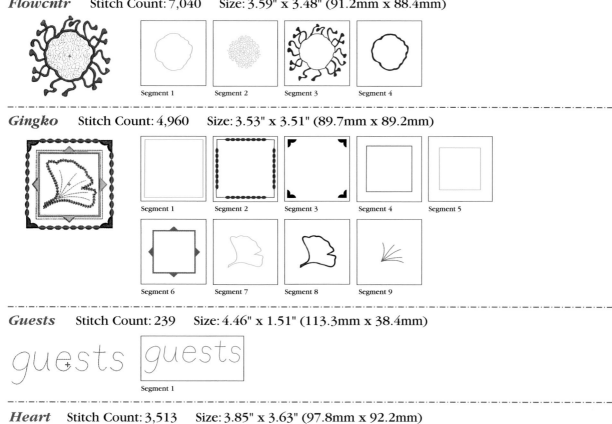

Segment 1   Segment 2   Segment 3   Segment 4

Segment 1   Segment 2   Segment 3   Segment 4   Segment 5

Segment 6   Segment 7   Segment 8   Segment 9

Guests   Stitch Count: 239   Size: 4.46" x 1.51" (113.3mm x 38.4mm)

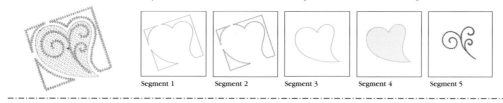

Segment 1

Heart   Stitch Count: 3,513   Size: 3.85" x 3.63" (97.8mm x 92.2mm)

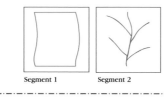

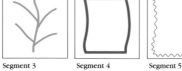

Segment 1   Segment 2   Segment 3   Segment 4   Segment 5

Modleaf   Stitch Count: 4,367   Size: 3.07" x 3.56" (77.9mm x 90.4mm)

Segment 1   Segment 2   Segment 3   Segment 4   Segment 5

Moon   Stitch Count: 2,733   Size: 3.20" x 3.62" (81.3mm x 92.0mm)

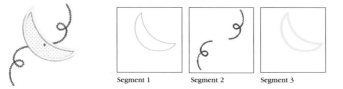

Segment 1   Segment 2   Segment 3

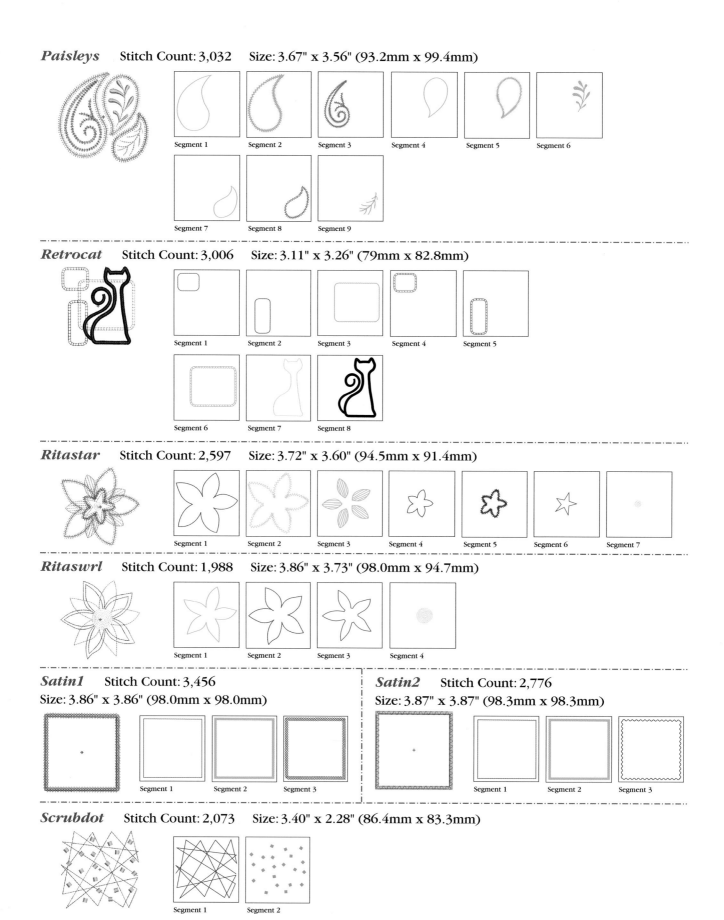

Paisleys   Stitch Count: 3,032   Size: 3.67" x 3.56" (93.2mm x 99.4mm)

Segment 1   Segment 2   Segment 3   Segment 4   Segment 5   Segment 6

Segment 7   Segment 8   Segment 9

Retrocat   Stitch Count: 3,006   Size: 3.11" x 3.26" (79mm x 82.8mm)

Segment 1   Segment 2   Segment 3   Segment 4   Segment 5

Segment 6   Segment 7   Segment 8

Ritastar   Stitch Count: 2,597   Size: 3.72" x 3.60" (94.5mm x 91.4mm)

Segment 1   Segment 2   Segment 3   Segment 4   Segment 5   Segment 6   Segment 7

Ritaswrl   Stitch Count: 1,988   Size: 3.86" x 3.73" (98.0mm x 94.7mm)

Segment 1   Segment 2   Segment 3   Segment 4

Satin1   Stitch Count: 3,456
Size: 3.86" x 3.86" (98.0mm x 98.0mm)

Segment 1   Segment 2   Segment 3

Satin2   Stitch Count: 2,776
Size: 3.87" x 3.87" (98.3mm x 98.3mm)

Segment 1   Segment 2   Segment 3

Scrubdot   Stitch Count: 2,073   Size: 3.40" x 2.28" (86.4mm x 83.3mm)

Segment 1   Segment 2

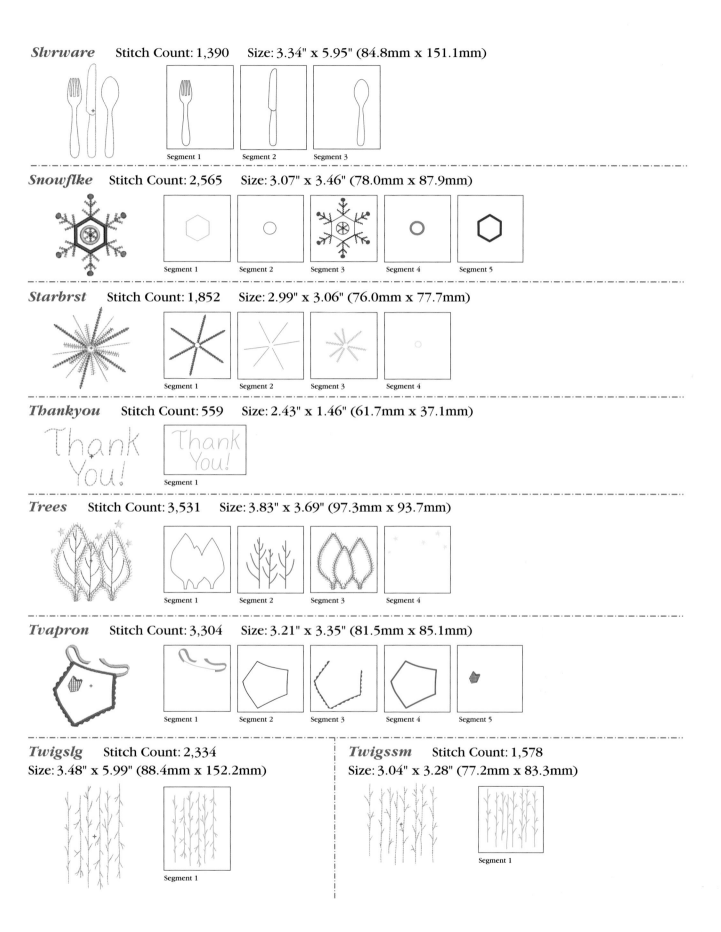

Slvrware   Stitch Count: 1,390   Size: 3.34" x 5.95" (84.8mm x 151.1mm)

Segment 1   Segment 2   Segment 3

Snowflke   Stitch Count: 2,565   Size: 3.07" x 3.46" (78.0mm x 87.9mm)

Segment 1   Segment 2   Segment 3   Segment 4   Segment 5

Starbrst   Stitch Count: 1,852   Size: 2.99" x 3.06" (76.0mm x 77.7mm)

Segment 1   Segment 2   Segment 3   Segment 4

Thankyou   Stitch Count: 559   Size: 2.43" x 1.46" (61.7mm x 37.1mm)

Segment 1

Trees   Stitch Count: 3,531   Size: 3.83" x 3.69" (97.3mm x 93.7mm)

Segment 1   Segment 2   Segment 3   Segment 4

Tvapron   Stitch Count: 3,304   Size: 3.21" x 3.35" (81.5mm x 85.1mm)

Segment 1   Segment 2   Segment 3   Segment 4   Segment 5

Twigslg   Stitch Count: 2,334
Size: 3.48" x 5.99" (88.4mm x 152.2mm)

Segment 1

Twigssm   Stitch Count: 1,578
Size: 3.04" x 3.28" (77.2mm x 83.3mm)

Segment 1

About Mary Mulari

Mary Mulari is a seasoned author and sought-after public speaker and teacher. Along with her busy production and traveling schedules, she has written 19 books, including *Made for Travel*, *Simply Napkins* with Gail Brown and *Embroidery Machine Essentials: Appliqué Techniques*. Mary displays her know-how as a guest on "Sewing with Nancy" (PBS television) and as a seminar presenter. She designs fabric collections for Marcus Brothers Textiles, machine embroidery appliqué designs for several companies and has her own pattern line. Her latest embroidery designs, a collaboration with Rita Farro, are called "Homemaking: 7 Days a Week" and feature redwork-style designs for dishtowels and making a house a home. From her home and office in Aurora, Minn., Mary stays connected with readers and audiences worldwide through her steadily growing body of work and her Web site www.marymulari.com.

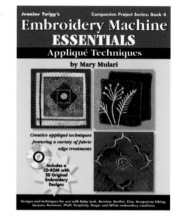

For more information on embroidery, purchase additional titles in this series: Embroidery Machine Essentials; More Embroidery Machine Essentials; Companion Project Series Book 1: Basic Techniques; Companion Project Series Book 2: Fleece Techniques; Companion Project Series Book 3: Quilting Techniques; and Companion Project Series Book 4: Appliqué Techniques.

How to Use the CD

The embroidery designs featured in this book are located on the CD. You must have a computer and compatible embroidery software to access and utilize the designs. Basic computer knowledge is helpful to understand how to copy the designs onto the hard-drive of your computer.

To access the designs, insert the CD into your computer. The designs are located on the CD in folders for each embroidery machine format. Copy the design files onto your computer using the computer operating system, embroidery design cataloging software, or open the designs directly into your equipment embroidery software. Be sure to copy only the embroidery design format compatible with your brand of embroidery equipment.

Once the designs have been loaded into software or saved on your computer, transfer the design to your embroidery machine following the manufacturer's instruction for your equipment. For more information about using these designs with your software or embroidery equipment, consult your owner's manual or seek advice from the dealer who honors your equipment warranty.